T0290215

Ask
and
Task

Questions and Activities for Communication Practice

Also by Nancy Ellen Zelman
Conversation Inspirations

Ask
and
Task

PHOTOCOPYABLE

Questions and Activities
for Communication Practice
Revised Edition

Nancy Ellen Zelman, esq.

Pro Lingua  Associates

Pro Lingua Associates, Publishers
74 Cotton Mill Hill, Suite A315
Brattleboro, Vermont 05301 USA
Office: 802-257-7779
Orders: 800-366- 4775
Email: info@ProLinguaAssociates.com
WebStore www.ProLinguaAssociates.com
SAN: 216-0579

At Pro Lingua
our objective is to foster an approach
to learning and teaching that we call
interplay, the interaction of language
learners and teachers with their materials,
with the language and culture,
and with each other in active, creative,
and productive play.

Copyright © 2016, 2020 Nancy Ellen Zelman

ISBN 13: 978-0-86647-503-7

All rights reserved. No part of this publication may be reproduced or transmitted in any form or by any means, digital, electronic, mechanical, photocopying, recording, or other, or stored in an information storage or retrieval system without permission in writing from the publisher. However, permission is granted by the publisher as follows:

Teachers may copy pages from *Ask and Task* for classroom use only.

This book was set in Palatino, designed originally in 1948 in Frankfurt by Hermann Zapf for the Linotype foundry. Although a modern, easy-to-read, calligraphic typeface, it is based on Renaissance designs typical of the Palatinate area of Germany. It was said to be the most widely used, and pirated, face of the twentieth century. This book was printed and bound by Gasch Printing in Odenton, Maryland. Cover art: green backgound © Vladamir Assylov, photo © Dmitriy Shironosov/Dreamstime.com. Title page © Imagincy/ Dreamstime.com. Book design RC Clark with AA Burrows. Cover AA Burrows.

Printed in the United States of America

Second, revised edition, sixth printing 2020. 3550 copies in print

User's Guide

This book is divided into two parts: Questions and Activities (Tasks). There are 40 topics with two or four pages of Questions and one page of Tasks for each topic. All the material is presented as sheets of photocopyable cards. The material is intended for use with English language learners at intermediate proficiency level, and it is best used with high school and adult groups. With some adaptation, however, the book can also be used with middle school students or with any groups who want conversation practice.

Both the questions and the tasks can be used in a wide variety of ways to facilitate learning. The questions are to prompt thought and conversation; the tasks are to promote language use while accomplishing some kind of project. You can use these cards cold, first going over the meaning of the question and any new vocabulary, or you can discuss each card to gauge the level of the students' ability to respond. Alternatively, you can introduce the topics using a separate related reading for each; this will help the students focus on the topic and give the students background to help form an opinion or carry out a task.

Prior to giving out the questions, you may prefer to present common vocabulary in the context of the topic, and have students create appropriate sentences using the new words. The students can then use this vocabulary while answering questions or completing tasks and can respond and perform better.

You will find different ways to use this book based on your own approach to teaching and your students' needs. To get you started, here are some ways I have used the cards:

Question Cards

1. Choose a topic and copy the two question sheets. Divide the students into pairs and give each student an A or B sheet. Have each pair ask and discuss their questions. You can listen in on groups and help the students or write down errors to be used in class at a later time.

2. Cut up a sheet and make a pile of cards. Put the students into small groups. One student in each group takes a card and asks the question; the students in the other group answer it. Alternatively, a student takes a card and answers the question, and the other students try to guess what the question is.

3. Put the students into small groups. One student silently reads a question card and whispers the question to the next student in the group as in the game "Telephone." The last person in the group announces the question.

4. Have the students prepare short individual speeches or presentations to the class based on their favorite question from the topic.

5. You or one of the students can dictate questions, and the students can discuss the questions in groups.

6. You can introduce vocabulary pertinent to the topics, and students in groups prepare answers to each question using the vocabulary. The group using the most new vocabulary wins.

7. You can use each question as a five-minute writing warmup before introducing the topic, or as a wrap-up at the end of the topic.

8. Have each student choose a question. Then have each student lead the class in a discussion of that question.

9. Hand out one question card to each student. On another blank card, each student write an answer to the question they were given. Divide the students into groups. Have all cards, questions and answers, turned face down and mixed, and the students play the matching game, finding the answers that match the questions.

10. Read some or all of the questions to one topic and have the class try to guess the topic until one student guesses the exact wording. Continue that on a daily basis for all the topics in the book. The student who guessed the most topics wins.

Task Cards

1. Many of these activities, called tasks, can be worked on as individual homework assignments. The students can present their tasks to the class and explain how they found their information and why they chose to include it.

2. Several students can be assigned the same task to do at home. During class they will work as a team and prepare a presentation explaining all their work.

3. You can divide the students into groups of three or four and have the students work on a specified part of a task either in class or at home. They can present their findings to the class as a team project.

4. You can choose one task and have all the students work together to complete it.

5. You can bring to class a completed task to use as a sample for the students. The students can decide what could be improved.

6. You can ask the students to create their own tasks. You can have the students work on these tasks at home and present them to the class.

7. The students can make up their own tasks, and you can write them separately on small folded papers. The students can then pick out a task and figure out what to do.

8. You can have a "fair" where tasks from the units are displayed for other classes or parents to view. Students can explain their tasks and what they learned.

9. You can display tasks and the class can guess which students completed which tasks.

10. Assign students a task and have the students make a presentation only explaining the steps they would take to do the task. The rest of the class can follow the steps and bring in their completed tasks.

11. Have the students look at the questions for the unit that corresponds to the tasks. Which questions can be used to complete a task?

12. Have the students make up a task and assign a student to complete it and then present it to the class.

Contents

Contents

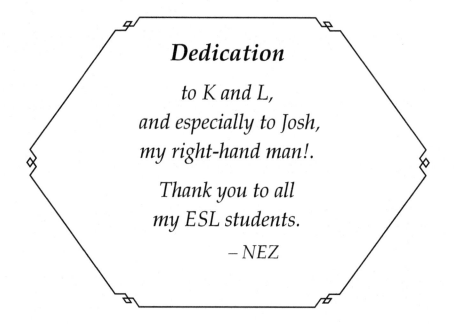

Dedication

to K and L,
and especially to Josh,
my right-hand man!.

Thank you to all
my ESL students.

– NEZ

A final introductory note:

The questions and activities presented in this book are merely suggestions for you to use to stimulate thoughtful and meaningful conversation. The most important thing to keep in mind as you use this book is to be flexible. Adapt the material to fit your students interests and abilities. If a topic is inappropriate or it is too easy or difficult, with a few changes you may make it work. For example, try dropping or rewriting some of the cards or changing the vocabulary or tenses used. In the User's Guide, I have made suggestions, but be free to invent your own ways of introducing, following up, and reinforcing the topics and language used. To meet the needs of your class, many of the tasks and questions may be used either for homework or in class. Most of all, have fun with this book and with your students. Only through a positive, uplifting experience will the students retain their new language skills. *NEZ*

ASK
AND
TASK

A Advertising/Marketing

Tasks, page 92

1. What do you want to know about a product before you buy it?

2. What kind of labeling attracts your attention? Why?

3. Do you look at the ingredients on labels in the supermarket? What do you look for ?

4. Do you enjoy watching commercials on TV?

5. Are there any jingles that you cannot get out of your head?

6. Do you like to taste test at stores?

7. Do you read the ads that come with your mail each week?

8. Is there any product that should not be advertised on TV?

9. Have you ever seen an infomercial? Have you ever bought anything from an infomercial?

10. Do you read advertisements left on your car windshield?

11. Have you ever received something valuable in the mail that you did not order? If you received something, would you keep it?

12. Did you ever purchase something online but when you received it, you didn't want it anymore?

 ProLinguaAssociates.com ◊ Photocopyable © 2020 Nancy Ellen Zelman

B   Advertising/Marketing *Tasks, page 92*

13. Do you think it is right for companies to target children in their advertising?	**19. How does advertising in the US differ from advertising in your native country?**
14. What kind of advertising is impossible for you to resist?	**20. Do you collect coupons? Why or not?**
15. Do you think 3 minutes of commercial time during the Superbowl should cost millions of dollars? Why or why not?	**21. How does the design of a web page influence potential customers?**
16. Are some products better advertised on TV? In a newspaper or magazine? On an infomercial? On a pop up?	**22. Do you check online to see how a product is reviewed before you buy it?**
17. Were you ever talked into buying something that you didn't need from a sales associate?	**23. Do you think ordinary people should be portrayed in advertisements, or is it better to have "perfect-looking" people?**
18. Do you like it when sales associates shower you with perfume at a store?	**24. Do you think it is right for a company to pay a celebrity to endorse a product?**

A Animals

1. Which animal makes the best pet?	7. Should the government spend our tax dollars on saving animals?
2. What animal do you look like?	8. If a pet is ill, how much money should you spend to save it?
3. Which animal is the most dangerous?	9. When do you put a pet to sleep?
4. Can we save endangered animals?	10. Should scientists experiment on animals?
5. Do you treat pets as members of the family?	11. When a pet dies, do you bury it? Where?
6. Why are some animals becoming extinct?	12. Why do groups such as PETA demonstrate against wearing furs?

QUESTIONS

ProLinguaAssociates.com ◇ Photocopyable © 2020 Nancy Ellen Zelman

B   Animals

13, Do animals have feelings?

14. Do animals love people?

15. Are animals intelligent?

16. Is it better to adopt a pet from the Humane Society or to buy one from a breeder?

17. Is it important to have a pet in the family?

18. How can pets teach children responsibility?

19. Why do some countries have so many stray dogs in the streets?

20. Why is it important to spay and neuter pets?

21. Is it the owner's responsibility if a pet bites a stranger?

22. Is it important to punish people who are maltreating pets?

23. Should Humane Societies do background checks to make sure a family has enough money to adopt an animal?

24. Is it wrong to feed wild animals?

QUESTIONS

A Appearance

QUESTIONS

1. What part of your body do you like the most?

2. What part of your body do you not like?

3. Would you ever consider plastic surgery to change your appearance?

4. In the summer, do you show off your body or cover it?

5. Do you ever wear hats?

6. What kind of T-shirts do you prefer?

7. How important is your appearance?

8. Do you feel comfortable in your clothes?

9. Do you feel good about your body?

10. Do you prefer long hair or short hair? Why?

11. Do you like the way you look in pictures?

12. Do you have any birthmarks? Where?

QUESTIONS

 ProLinguaAssociates.com ◇ Photocopyable © 2020 Nancy Ellen Zelman

B   Appearance

Tasks, page 94

QUESTIONS

13. Do you have any scars?

14. Do you have any tattoos? If you got one, what would it be?

15. How can you improve your appearance?

16. What impression do you think your appearance makes on others?

17. Would you ever go to a nudist camp or a nude beach? Why or why not?

18. Is there anything you want to change about your spouse's appearance? Your children's?

19. Do you judge others by their appearance? How?

20. Would you hire someone who has a shaved head, multiple piercings, and tattoos over their body and face? Why?

21. Do you like to use makeup?

22. Do you have a mustache or beard?

23. Would you ever shave your head?

24. Would you prefer to have a bald spot or wear a hair-piece or wig?

QUESTIONS

A Beliefs

QUESTIONS

1. Do you believe in life after death?	7. Do you believe in guardian angels?
2. Do you believe in the goodness of people?	8. Do you believe in fate?
3. Do you have a faith you believe in?	9. Do you believe in a supernatural being?
4. Do you believe in true love?	10. Do you trust modern medicine?
5. Do you believe in reincarnation?	11. Do you believe in faith healing?
6. Do you believe in miracles?	12. Do you believe in our government?

 ProLinguaAssociates.com ◇ Photocopyable © 2020 Nancy Ellen Zelman

B   Beliefs

Tasks, page 95

13. Do you believe in superstitions?	**19. Do you believe in ghosts?**
14. Do you believe in luck?	**20. Do you believe monogamy is natural for humans?**
15. Do you believe in psychics?	**21. Do you believe in love at first sight?**
16. Do you believe in the institution of marriage?	**22. Do you believe in gut instincts?**
17. Do you believe there is life on other planets?	**23. Do you believe in evolution?**
18. Do you believe in sex before marriage?	**24. Do you believe in coincidence?**

A Business

QUESTIONS

1. Is it better to be the owner or a manager of a business? Who has more headaches?

2. Are there any businesses you would want to run? Any that you would not?

3. What businesses have been affected by outsourcing?

4. What is the best country to outsource to?

5. Would you pay more money to buy something made in this country rather than another country?

6. Would you buy something if you knew that the people making it were children?

7. Would you want to employ your family in your business?

8. Would it be easy or difficult to run a business with a spouse? Children?

9. How long would you work at a job before asking for a raise?

10. Would you prefer to hire someone you know or someone you don't?

11. What would you do if you knew someone in your business was stealing?

12. If you were short of money, would you ask for an advance on your salary?

ProLinguaAssociates.com ◊ Photocopyable © 2020 Nancy Ellen Zelman

B Business

QUESTIONS

13. What are some ways to find a job? Are these ways different in your country?

14. Is a high school education important for finding a job? A college education?

15. How do people learn a trade in your country?

16. Which jobs are the easiest to get in your country? In the US?

17. How do you "dress for success"?

18. Can you really control the "first impression" you make on employers?

19. How important is networking in finding a job?

20. What kinds of jobs can you find online? What kinds of jobs are not advertised online?

21. What are some ways you can increase employee productivity?

22. What are some ways to increase sales in a business?

23. How much money are you willing to invest in a business?

24. Would you prefer to get stocks in a company or money?

Photocopyable © 2020 Nancy Ellen Zelman ◇ ProLinguaAssociates.com

A Cars and Drivers

QUESTIONS

1. Do you use a GPS or do you ask people for directions if you are lost?

2. Do you know how to fix a flat tire?

3. Do you carry a first aid kit in your car?

4. Did you did ever get carsick?

5. Do you prefer to be a passenger or a driver?

6. Do you sing in your vehicle?

7. Do you prefer to listen to the radio or your own playlist?

8. Do you ever look at other drivers when you are in a car?

9. Did you ever experience road rage? What happened? What did you do?

10. If someone is injured on the road do you get out of your vehicle and try to help?

11. Have you ever called in an accident?

12. What is the best car on the market for you?

QUESTIONS

 ProLinguaAssociates.com ◊ Photocopyable © 2020 Nancy Ellen Zelman

QUESTIONS (left margin)

13. Do you honk the horn to annoy people? To say hello?	19. Are you a back seat driver?
14. Do you like classic cars? Which ones?	20. Would you be able to teach your teenager how to drive?
15. What is the fastest speed you have ever driven? Why did you drive that fast?	21. Are women better drivers than men?
16. Do you ever let your children steer the car?	22. What age group are the most dangerous drivers?
17. Do you always wear your seat belt?	23. Should there be a maximum age to drive for seniors?
18. Do you stop at yellow lights or do you speed through them?	24. Do you ever drive in the carpool lane even when you have no passengers?

QUESTIONS (right margin)

A Chores

1. What is your favorite household chore?	7. Do you wash the windows in your house? How often?
2. What products make cleaning your house easier?	8. What chores do you ask others to do?
3. What cleaning tool could you not live without?	9. Do others perform chores as well as you do?
4. How long does it take you to clean your house?	10. What chores do you dread?
5. Do you garden? How much time do you spend on it?	11. Who runs the errands in your home?
6. What is the worst part of working in your yard?	12. What is the one appliance you could not live without?

      ProLinguaAssociates.com ◊ Photocopyable © 2020 Nancy Ellen Zelman

B Chores

13. How do you divide the cooking and cleaning dishes chores?	19. Are there any chores that no one does in your house?
14. Do you feel that one person in your household does more chores than the others?	20. How many loads of laundry do you do each week?
15. Is it important to clean your room every day?	21. Do you cook? Why or why not?
16. Who does the vacuuming in your house? The dusting?	22. How often do you clean your house?
17. Do you pay others to do chores for you?	23. Do you disinfect electronic devices?
18. Which chores do you need help with?	24. Are there any chores that you do in the US that you wouldn't do in your country?

A Communication

Tasks, page 99

QUESTIONS

1. Do you write letters to anyone?

2. What is the most effective way to communicate with your relatives?

3. How do you communicate with friends in your native country?

4. Do you speak any other languages besides your native language and English?

5. What is the most important language to speak if you want to travel?

6. Why do we call the mail we post "snail mail"? Do you still use it?

7. What is the best way to tell someone bad news? What is the best way to tell someone good news?

8. Do you know sign language? Do you know anyone who does?

9. Do you think men are better communicators than women?

10. How do you communicate with babies?

11. Do you have a cell phone? Why do/don't you need one?

12. Do you have a home phone? Why do/don't you need one?

QUESTIONS

  ProLinguaAssociates.com ◊ Photocopyable © 2020 Nancy Ellen Zelman

Q U E S T I O N S

13. Have you ever lied and told someone there was a bad connection just to get off the phone?

14. Have you ever hung up on anyone? Has anyone ever hung up on you?

15. How do you feel when you call a business and a recording answers the phone?

16. How many minutes is the longest time you will remain on hold before hanging up?

17. Do you have an answering machine? What is the message?

18. Do you have caller ID? Why/why not?

19. Do you send greeting cards to loved ones?

20. How much time do you spend texting?

21. Do you text when friends are talking to you?

22. Do you use emojis when you text? Which are your favorites?

23. Do you think it is rude when people talk loudly on their phones in public?

24. Do you check your messages when you are out with others?

Q U E S T I O N S

A Crime/Punishment

Tasks, page 100

Q U E S T I O N S

1. In what ways is capital punishment fair?

2. How can we ever be sure of a person's guilt?

3. Does prison rehabilitate prisoners?

4. Should prison inmates have privileges? Which ones?

5. What can be done to reduce overcrowding in prisons?

6. Should sexual predators be allowed back in society after serving time?

7. Why would some people want to commit suicide?

8. Do you think suing someone is the best way to resolve differences?

9. Did you ever sue anyone?

10. Do you believe in the "three strikes" law?

11. Should medical or recreational marijuana be legal in all states?

12. Are children exploited in the US for work or sex?

Q U E S T I O N S

  ProLinguaAssociates.com ◊ Photocopyable © 2020 Nancy Ellen Zelman

QUESTIONS

13. Why are children exploited in some countries?	19. Do too many police officers use excessive force?
14. Should prostitutes or johns be punished as severely as pimps?	20. Should there be police with guns on all airplanes? In schools? At businesses?
15. How well are traffic laws followed in your native country?	21. Do police treat all races equally?
16. What do you think of traffic cameras?	22. Should a homeowner be allowed to kill an intruder?
17. Are you afraid of the police or do you like to see them?	23. Have you ever protested or taken part in a strike?
18. Have you ever called the police? Why?	24. Have you ever been pulled over by the police?

1. Will there ever be peace in the Middle East?	7. What do you think of the American political system?
2. Is there enough security at airports? In other public places? On the internet?	8. Do you think our President is doing a good job domestically?
3. Should the government be allowed to spy on citizens?	9. How is the President doing in world affairs?
4. Do the police target people based on race?	10. What are some problems between the US and other countries? What can be done about them?
5. What should the US do with the children coming across the border illegally and alone?	11. Can the US trust other countries? Which ones?
6. Are children used as slaves in some parts of the world?	12. Are schools dangerous in the US? Why are there school shootings?

QUESTIONS

QUESTIONS

13. How can you avoid road rage?	19. Should the US trade political prisoners? How should we decide which ones?
14. Is the UN useful in solving problems between countries?	20. Should the US give political asylum to people who are experiencing religious persecution? Racial persecution? Gender persecution? Sexual preference persecution?
15. How can food producers ensure that our food is safe to eat?	21. What should be the role of the President's spouse?
16. Should the federal government provide health insurance? What other services should it provide?	22. Is a politician's private sex life important to constituents? Should it be?
17. How can the world stop the spread of deadly viruses from becoming pandemics?	23. Do politicians get paid enough money? Too much?
18. Should the US intervene in other countries' problems?	24. Is there ever a good reason to seek out and assassinate another country's political leader?

QUESTIONS

A   Customs/Holidays

Tasks, page 102

QUESTIONS

1. What is one custom you brought to the US from your native country?

2. Are holidays in the US similar to those in your native country?

3. Do you have a "Thanksgiving" in your country?

4. What do people in your country eat at holidays?

5. How do people in your native country celebrate a wedding?

6. What do people in your native country do at funerals?

7. What do people in your native country wear to celebrate their heritage?

8. What kinds of dances do people in your country perform?

9. Is dancing similar in your country to dancing here in the US?

10. Are there any holidays we have in the US that involve your country in one way or another?

11. What does a typical festive meal in your country consist of?

12. Do you celebrate American holidays? Which ones?

QUESTIONS

   ProLinguaAssociates.com ◇ Photocopyable © 2020 Nancy Ellen Zelman

QUESTIONS

13. What are the national holidays in your native country?	19. Are there any holidays in your native country when people give or are given money?
14. Do you have parades in your native country?	20. Do you and your family have any special traditions based on the calendar?
15. Do people or organizations sponsor floats in your country?	21. What are some traditional songs from your country? When are they sung?
16. How do people celebrate New Year's Eve in your country?	22. Are there patriotic displays at sporting events in your country?
17. Do you have Mother's Day and Father's Day? What do children in your country do on those days?	23. The colors of the US flag are red, white, and blue. What are the colors of your native country's flag? Can you explain why they were chosen?
18. Is there a holiday you do not enjoy? Why?	24. Is there one religion that dominates your country? How does that religion influence customs and holidays?

QUESTIONS

A Daily Rituals

Tasks, page 103

1. What time do you get up every morning?

2. What is the first thing you do after you get up?

3. Do you comb or brush your hair?

4. Do you make your own breakfast?

5. What do you have for breakfast?

6. How do you choose the clothes you wear in the morning?

7. Do you usually get to work/school on time?

8. How much time do you spend at work/school?

9. Do you socialize with your coworkers or classmates after school?

10. Do you have any breaks at work or school?

11. How many meals do you usually eat each day?

12. What do you have for snacks during the day?

 ProLinguaAssociates.com ◊ Photocopyable © 2020 Nancy Ellen Zelman

B   Daily Rituals

Tasks, page 103

13. Where do you usually eat your lunch?	19. Where do you get your hair cut?
14. How do you get home from work /school?	20. Do you ever get facials? Manicures? Pedicures?
15. What do you do when you get home from your day at work/school?	21. When was the last time you got a massage?
16. At the end of the day, what do you do with the clothes you wore that day?	22. What do you do before you go to bed every night?
17. Do you usually take a bath or shower? When?	23. How much exercise do you get every day?
18. How often do you cut your nails?	24. How much time do you spend on the computer each day?

Photocopyable © 2020 Nancy Ellen Zelman ◇ ProLinguaAssociates.com

A Dating/Marriage

Tasks, page 104

1. What are some questions you would ask if you did speed dating?

2. How does dating differ in the US and in your native country?

3. Would you pay a matchmaker to find your match?

4. What is the best way to meet a prospective mate?

5. What are the best online dating sites?

6. What is one wedding custom that you do not like in this country or in your native country?

7. Do people get engaged in your native country? For how long?

8. What are some characteristics you would like to find in a mate? A mother-in-law?

9. Is there an age in which a person is considered an "old maid" in your country? Is there an age for a "confirmed bachelor"?

10. What is the best age for marriage?

11. How does your culture look upon unmarried men and women who cohabitate?

12. How much age difference is acceptable between a man and a woman for dating or marriage?

 ProLinguaAssociates.com ◊ Photocopyable © 2020 Nancy Ellen Zelman

B   Dating/Marriage

Tasks, page 104

13. What do you think of "Cougars"? "Sugar daddies"?

14. Is financial security more important than love in a marriage?

15. Can you learn to love someone?

16. Is it OK to break up by email or text?

17. What do you do with an ex who refuses to stop calling?

18. Is it important to have your family's approval when choosing a partner?

19. How important is it for you to marry someone of the same color? Religion?

20. Are marriages better when the partners have similar or opposite personalities?

21. What do you think of "blind dates"?

22. What do you think of hiring a surrogate if a woman is infertile? What do you think of international adoption?

23. At what age do boys and girls start having sex in your native country?

24. Is retaining virginity until marriage important?

A Death

QUESTIONS

1. Is suicide acceptable in your native country? When?

2. Would you fill out a Do Not Resuscitate form for the hospital? Why or why not?

3. If someone is suffering, would you help them die?

4. Is it ever a good idea to take someone off life support?

5. Is it OK to euthanize unwanted animals?

6. Why is it illegal to euthanize people?

7. Is there a difference between "pulling the plug" and euthanizing?

8. What is "suicide by cop?" Do you have that in your native country?

9. Why do people commit suicide? Is it a cowardly action? Why?

10. Is suicide ever a heroic action?

11. Should the financial situation of a person be considered when deciding the fate of someone who is terminally ill?

12. What is the best age at which to die?

B   Death

Tasks, page 105

13. What do you believe happens to people when they die?	19. Why do many families take their loved ones home to die?
14. Have you ever wanted to communicate with someone who has died? What would you say?	20. If you had control over where you died, where would you want to die?
15. Do you think some people can communicate with the dead? Have you ever tried?	21. Do you want your body buried? Cremated?
16. If you could be reincarnated, in what form would you like to return to life?	22. Would you want anyone to view your body?
17. Are we destined to die at a certain time? Can that time be changed?	23. Would you prefer to die in a hospital or at home?
18. Are you afraid of dying or death? Why?	24. How would you like your tombstone to read?

A Education

1. How much schooling does a person need?	7. How do schools in the US compare with schools from your native country?
2. What are the most important subjects in school?	8. Should parents be punished if their children are absent from school without permission?
3. Is a good education important for success?	9. How would you change schools in your country? This country?
4. Is it better to go to a private school or a public school?	10. How many students should there be in a class?
5. Is it best to be home schooled?	11. How can parents help their children in school?
6. Which subjects are not important for your future?	12. Should schools have longer or shorter hours?

 ProLinguaAssociates.com ◊ Photocopyable © 2020 Nancy Ellen Zelman

Tasks, page 106

13. Is it better to have a three-month vacation or should schools have classes all year?	19. Are you ever too old to go back to school?
14. Should all education be free? Up to what grade?	20. Would you prefer to be a student or a teacher?
15. Are teachers paid enough?	21. Which is more important, school and book learning or experience in the outside world?
16. Should teachers have guns at school?	22. Do schools do enough to help students with learning difficulties?
17. Which is more important to have in a classroom, books or computers?	23. How should students be punished for misbehaving in school?
18. In your native country, until what age is education compulsory?	24. Do schools do enough to protect students against bullying?

Photocopyable © 2020 Nancy Ellen Zelman ◇ ProLinguaAssociates.com

QUESTIONS

1. What can we do to preserve our environment?	7. Are people causing global warming or is it inevitable?
2. What do people do to pollute the environment?	8. Is there anything people can do to slow global warming?
3. Is there more pollution in this country than in your native country?	9. How does pollution affect our health?
4. Is recycling important to you? How do you recycle?	10. How do tourists help or hurt the environment they visit?
5. Is recycling important in your native country? Why or why not?	11. What is happening to our beaches? Can we do anything to protect our beaches?
6. How does pollution affect our environment?	12. How can people be educated to be more environmentally aware?

QUESTIONS

QUESTIONS

13. Is there a lot of litter in the streets in this country? Is there litter in your native country?	19. Why is China the biggest contributor to CO_2 emissions?
14. Can people adapt to climate change?	20. Is it important to protect animals from extinction?
15. Are there more natural disasters in this country than in your native country?	21. What are poachers? Should poachers be punished? How?
16. What are some incentives the government can use to induce companies to reduce pollution?	22. What nature preserves have you visited?
17. Would you spend more money to drive a more gas efficient car?	23. Are there any insects/ animals you would like to see extinct? Why?
18. How can we prepare for natural disasters?	24. Are any animals eaten in your native country that are not eaten in the US?

QUESTIONS

A Family

1. How many brothers and sisters do you have?	7. What do you call your mother-in-law and your father-in-law?
2. Do you have a lot of cousins?	8. How often do you get together with your in-laws?
3. Do you prefer to get together with your immediate family or your extended family?	9. When your extended family gets together, where do you meet?
4. Are your parents alive? How old are they?	10. What kinds of activities do you do with your family?
5. Do you have grandparents? Great-grandparents?	11. Do you have any friends that you treat as family?
6. Do your in-laws ever criticize you?	12. Who in your family needs the most attention?

QUESTIONS

   ProLinguaAssociates.com   ◇   Photocopyable © 2020 Nancy Ellen Zelman

B Family

Tasks, page 108

13. What is your family's biggest celebration?	19. Who does most of the cooking in your family?
14. What traditions does your family pass down from generation to generation?	20. Who makes the biggest mess in your family?
15. Does your family have any secret family recipes?	21. What family event will you always remember?
16. Do you ever have squabbles at family events?	22. What games do you and your family enjoy playing together?
17. What does your family usually fight about?	23. What role do you play in your family?
18. What language do you and your family speak when you are together?	24. Which job is more important, wife or mother? Husband or father?

QUESTIONS

Photocopyable © 2020 Nancy Ellen Zelman ◊ ProLinguaAssociates.com

A Fashion

QUESTIONS

1. Where do you usually buy your clothes?	7. Do you get hand-me-down clothes for your children from friends or relatives?
2. Do you buy clothes for other people in your family?	8. Would you buy your clothes at a second-hand store?
3. How much do you spend on clothing each month?	9. What kind of clothes would you never buy at a thrift store?
4. What is the most expensive item you ever bought for yourself? For someone else?	10. What are some clothes you would never wear?
5. What do you do with clothes you do not wear anymore?	11. Do you look for brand names when you buy clothing? Which ones?
6. Did you ever wear hand-me-down clothes as a child?	12. Is brand name clothing better than generic clothing?

QUESTIONS

B   Fashion

Tasks, page 109

13. Do you like to wear stylish clothes?	19. Do you like to wear colorful clothing or do you like to blend in?
14. How do you find out which styles are in or out?	20. How often do you check yourself in the mirror before you leave for the day?
15. How often do you clean out your closets?	21. Is there a famous person whose wardrobe you wish you had?
16. Have you ever worn inappropriate clothing to an event?	22. What colors best suit you?
17. Do you make sure all your clothes match before you go out?	23. How do your clothes mirror how you feel about yourself?
18. Do you buy patterns? Plaids? Polka dots?	24. Do you know any famous designers or models?

A Favorites

1. What is your favorite snack?	7. What is your favorite dessert?
2. What is your favorite fruit or vegetable?	8. What is your favorite country? State?
3. What is your favorite ice cream flavor?	9. What is your favorite TV show?
4. What is your favorite color?	10. What is your favorite video game?
5. Who is your favorite actor? Singer?	11. What is your favorite website?
6. Who is your favorite artist? Composer?	12. What is your favorite American holiday?

QUESTIONS

QUESTIONS

 ProLinguaAssociates.com ◇ Photocopyable © 2020 Nancy Ellen Zelman

B Favorites

13. What is your favorite food?	19. What is your favorite hobby?
14. What is your favorite school subject?	20. What is your favorite flower?
15. Who is your favorite TV character?	21. What is your favorite animal?
16. Who is your favorite literary character?	22. What is your favorite make of car?
17. What is your favorite book or poem?	23. What is your favorite drink?
18. Who is your favorite author?	24. Who is your favorite anime or cartoon character?

Photocopyable © 2020 Nancy Ellen Zelman ◊ ProLinguaAssociates.com

A Food

1. Do you enjoy cooking?	7. Which fruits do you like/ dislike?
2. What is one food you cannot stand the smell of?	8. Do you go out to eat often? Where do you go?
3. What kind of ethnic food do you like?	9. What is your favorite restaurant? Why?
4. Do you read the labels on food products before you put them your cart?	10. Have you ever sent your food back at a restaurant?
5. Have you ever grown your own food? What did you grow?	11. Did you ever argue with the waiter about the bill?
6. What vegetables do you like/dislike?	12. Did you ever not have sufficient funds to pay a restaurant or grocery bill? What did you do?

QUESTIONS QUESTIONS

 ProLinguaAssociates.com ◇ Photocopyable © 2020 Nancy Ellen Zelman

13. Do you bag your own groceries? Why?	19. Do you buy organic food? Do you think it is healthier than non-organic food?
14. Do you cut coupons or look online for discounts?	20. Do you have any dietary restrictions?
15. Which food could you not live without?	21. Do you eat at fast food restaurants? Which ones?
16. What food do you force yourself to eat? Why?	22. Are there fast food restaurants in your native country? Which ones?
17. Is there any food you can't stop eating once you start?	23. What do you usually order when you eat at a restaurant?
18. How do you make sure you are eating healthily?	24. If someone asks you to taste a food and you do not like it, do you tell the truth?

QUESTIONS

A Gender/Sex

QUESTIONS

1. Which gender is more emotionally detached?	7. Can sexual identity be changed?
2. Which gender cooks better?	8. Why do women live longer than men?
3. Which gender is physically stronger?	9. Do men and women react differently to pain?
4. What are some ways men and women think differently?	10. Are men more competitive than women?
5. Who is a better friend, a man or a woman?	11. Do men and women feel love in the same way?
6. Is sexual orientation determined at birth?	12. Which gender makes the better parent?

ProLinguaAssociates.com ◊ Photocopyable © 2020 Nancy Ellen Zelman

Tasks, page 112

13. What qualities are innately female? Male?	**19.** Why do women strive to look young as long as they can? Do men do this?
14. Is it as important for a woman as it is for a man to find a job?	**20.** What are your favorite girls' names? Boys' names?
15. At what age is a woman considered "over the hill"? What is the age for a man?	**21.** What are some jobs that are fit only for women? Men? Why?
16. What do you think of men who stay at home while their wives work outside the home?	**22.** Are all men hunters? In what ways?
17. Do homosexual partners make good parents?	**23.** Are all women gatherers? How?
18. When do you explain sexuality to a child?	**24.** If you could have only one child, would you prefer a girl or a boy?

QUESTIONS QUESTIONS

A Health

1. Do you exercise regularly?	7. Are you afraid of hospitals?
2. Do you need to join a gym to exercise?	8. Did you ever break a bone? What happened?
3. Do you need to have a partner to keep up a regular exercise routine?	9. Do you believe in holistic medicine?
4. Do you eat balanced meals?	10. Have you ever visited an acupuncturist?
5. Do you have a doctor you see regularly? Do you trust your doctor?	11. Do you believe in home remedies?
6. Do you always tell your doctor the truth about your health and habits?	12. Do you take any vitamins or food supplements? Which ones? Why?

QUESTIONS

QUESTIONS

ProLinguaAssociates.com ◊ Photocopyable © 2020 Nancy Ellen Zelman

13. Do you see the doctor when you feel sick or do you generally wait a few days?	19. Have you ever rushed anyone to the emergency room?
14. Did you ever want to be a doctor or a nurse?	20. Do you donate your blood?
15. Would you see a psychologist if you had emotional problems?	21. Which pain is worse, emotional or physical?
16. How often do you visit the dentist?	22. Do you have any allergies?
17. Is your oral health as important to you as the health of the rest of your body?	23. Do you know anyone struggling with dementia?
18. Do you know how to do CPR?	24. Have you ever struggled with anorexia or bulimia?

A Home

Tasks, page 114

1. Do you own your own home?

2. Do you keep valuables in your house?

3. Do you keep an extra key to your house in a secret place?

4. Do you enjoy decorating your home?

5. Where do you shop when you need something for your home?

6. What things do you have in your home that you cherish?

7. Do you have furniture you inherited from your ancestors?

8. Where do you keep your important papers?

9. What do you like to collect? Where do you keep your collection?

10. Does your house reflect your taste?

11. Do you take pride in keeping your house tidy? Clean?

12. Which do you prefer, modern or antique styles?

QUESTIONS

13. When you need to change something in your home, do you ask anyone to help you?

14. What is your favorite room in the house? Why?

15. How do pets affect the look of your house?

16. Do you prefer living in the city, the country, or the suburbs? Why?

17. Do you know your neighbors? Is that important to you?

18. Do you know where everything is in your house?

19. What do you commonly lose in your home? Where do you eventually find it?

20. Do you have a "junk" drawer? What is in it?

21. Does your house have "curbside appeal"?

22. Are you proud of your yard?

23. How often do you entertain at your house?

24. Would you prefer living in a house, apartment, or condo?

A Issues 1

Tasks, page 115

1. What is the most important current issue in this country?

2. What is the most important current issue in your country?

3. Is the US really a democracy?

4. Are political parties necessary?

5. Should religion be separated from government?

6. How and when should people participate in civil disobedience?

7. Should abortion be legal?

8. Do we need new marijuana laws?

9. Should there be a limit on the age of Supreme Court justices ?

10. Do we need to revise immigration laws?

11. Why are our prisons overcrowded?

12. Is full employment a possibility?

 ProLinguaAssociates.com ◊ Photocopyable © 2020 Nancy Ellen Zelman

B Issues 1

Tasks, page 115

13. What is the best way to select the leader of a country?	**19.** How well are we dealing with terrorism?
14. Is profiling by police widespread?	**20.** Is airport security working?
15. Is a sales tax fairer than income tax?	**21.** Should we have tougher gun laws?
16. Why do people join unions?	**22.** Should there be a minimum wage? What should it be?
17. Is political corruption widespread in this country?	**23.** What do you think about England's royalty?
18. Do you believe in a draft system for military service?	**24.** Could you be a hero if you think you see someone in immediate danger?

QUESTIONS

QUESTIONS

1. Is stem cell research necessary?

2. Does acupuncture really work?

3. Do you believe in holistic medicine?

4. Would you have plastic surgery?

5. Do fad diets work?

6. Are donor eggs for infertile couples a good thing?

7. Are you in favor of genetic engineering?

8. Is cloning morally acceptable?

9. What is your position on abortion?

10. Is there any good argument against birth control?

11. Are parents responsible for a child's obesity?

12. What can we do about the high cost of prescription drugs?

QUESTIONS

B   Issues 2

Tasks, page 115

13. How do you feel about seeing a Physician's Assistant and not the Doctor?	**19. Why does pornography exist?**
14. Is weight loss surgery a good idea?	**20. Why is online dating so popular in the US?**
15. How do you feel about polygamy?	**21. How do you feel about sex before marriage?**
16. How do feel about divorce?	**22. What is your opinion about having fathers in the delivery room?**
17. Which is better, open or closed adoption?	**23. What is your opinion about home birth with a midwife?**
18. What's your position on same sex marriage?	**24. Should we legalize prostitution?**

QUESTIONS

QUESTIONS

A   Least Favorites

Tasks, page 110

1. What is your least favorite animal smell?	7. Who is your least favorite celebrity?
2. What is your least favorite personality trait you find in others?	8. Who is your least favorite politician?
3. What is your least favorite personality trait in yourself?	9. Which is your least favorite day of the week?
4. What is your least favorite type of music?	10. Which is your least favorite color?
5. What is your least favorite time of day?	11. Which is your least favorite season?
6. What is your least favorite meal? Why?	12. What was your least favorite subject in school?

 ProLinguaAssociates.com ◊ Photocopyable © 2020 Nancy Ellen Zelman

B Least Favorites

Tasks, page 110

13. What was your least favorite movie?	19. What is your least favorite popular song?
14. What was your least favorite of the books you had to read for school?	20. What is your least favorite sport to watch? To play?
15. What is your least favorite insect?	21. What is your least favorite physical exercise?
16. What is your least favorite museum?	22. What is your least favorite vacation spot?
17. What is your least favorite TV show?	23. What is your least favorite amusement park?
18. Who is your least favorite comedian?	24. What is your least favorite question on this page?

QUESTIONS

QUESTIONS

Photocopyable © 2020 Nancy Ellen Zelman ◊ ProLinguaAssociates.com

A Love

1. Is there such a thing as love at first sight?	7. What is the difference between love and lust?
2. What is the most important quality in a potential mate?	8. Does a potential mate need to ask permission from the parents before marriage?
3. Can a person fall out of love? How?	9. How long should an engagement last?
4. How old do you have to be to be in love?	10. What is the best place to go for a honeymoon?
5. Do opposites attract?	11. What is the best way to meet a mate in this country?
6. Is there really only one person who is right for you?	12. How much should a couple spend on a wedding?

QUESTIONS

QUESTIONS

 ProLinguaAssociates.com ◊ Photocopyable © 2020 Nancy Ellen Zelman

B   Love

Tasks, page 116

13. Is it more important to buy an expensive wedding dress or to save the money?	19. Why do people cheat on their spouses?
14. How long is too long to date a person?	20. Could you forgive your spouse for cheating?
15. Should people live together before marriage?	21. Which is worse, emotional or physical infidelity?
16. Can money buy love?	22. Would you ever hire a wedding planner? Why?
17. How many children make the ideal family?	23. What is the most difficult part about getting married?
18. Which sex cheats more, men or women?	24. Would you renew your wedding vows?

Photocopyable © 2020 Nancy Ellen Zelman ◊ ProLinguaAssociates.com

A Money/Finance

Tasks, page 117

1. How important is money in your life?	7. Do you check your pay stubs?
2. Have you ever won any money?	8. Do you pick up change you see in the street?
3. Did you ever charge someone too much money for something?	9. Do you make a budget each month? Do you follow it?
4. How much money do you usually carry with you?	10. Do you like to gamble?
5. Do you pay for purchases with cash, cards, or checks?	11. Are you able to save money each week? What are you saving it for?
6. Do you always review your bills and statements before you pay them?	12. Do you give your children an allowance?

QUESTIONS

ProLinguaAssociates.com ◊ Photocopyable © 2020 Nancy Ellen Zelman

QUESTIONS

13. How old should children be in order to spend their own money?	19. How much money do you spend on living expenses each month?
14. What is the best way to invest your money?	20. Should the minimum wage be raised?
15. Do you know your credit score?	21. Did you ever lend a friend or relative any money? What happened?
16. What do you do when you are unable to pay a bill?	22. Do you give any money to charities or religious organizations?
17. Have you ever borrowed money from a family member?	23. Do you ever give money to beggars? Why or why not?
18. Would you ever pawn something you own to get cash?	24. If you had no job, would you beg on the street?

A   Native Country 1

Tasks, page 118

1. In what ways do you prefer the US to your native country?

2. In what ways do you prefer your native country to other countries?

3. Do many people from your native country emigrate to the US? Why?

4. What do you miss the most about your native country?

5. Who in your native country do you miss the most?

6. What is the best way to communicate with friends and family in your native country?

7. How does the government in the US differ from the government in your native country?

8. Are you afraid of the police in your native country?

9. Are there organizations to protect animals in your native country?

10. How does your native country protect the environment?

11. Is education important in your native country?

12. Is higher education affordable in your country?

B   Native Country 1

Tasks, page 118

13. What are the racial minorities in your country? Are the minorities and the majority treated equally?	19. Do people in your country have faith in the hospitals?
14. Are there gangs in your country? Crime lords?	20. What should a tourist see and do in your country?
15. What are the fast foods offered in your native country?	21. Is there anywhere in your country a tourist should avoid?
16. Is corruption common in your country?	22. How much money does a tourist need for a week in your country?
17. In your country, where do poor people live?	23. Is there any food in your native country that a tourist should avoid eating?
18. Are there old age homes in your country?	24. What is the currency in your country? What is the exhange rate?

A Native Country 2

1. Who is the most famous person in your country?	7. Do beggars ask for food or money in your country?
2. How do people show respect for others in your native country?	8. What are the best jobs in your country?
3. Do people earn enough money to live well in your country?	9. Where is the best place to live in your country?
4. Are bribes accepted in your country?	10. Are there social classes in your native country?
5. Is there a minimum wage in your country? What is it?	11. Are there different religions in your country?
6. Are children exploited in your native country?	12. How do people treat animals in your native country?

QUESTIONS

ProLinguaAssociates.com ◊ Photocopyable © 2020 Nancy Ellen Zelman

QUESTIONS

13. Does your country produce a lot of lawyers? Do people settle arguments through the courts?	19. What laws in your native country do you not like and why?
14. Is it difficult to get a divorce in your country?	20. Why do people from your native country come to the US? Why did you?
15. Is abortion available in your country?	21. What kind of games do children or adults play in your country?
16. In your country, are people patriotic?	22. In your country, are there any museums displaying historical artifacts?
17. How do people show their support for the government?	23. Is your country famous for any type of crafts?
18. How do people show they do not support government policy?	24. Are there any subjects that cannot be discussed openly and in public in your country?

QUESTIONS

A The News

QUESTIONS

1. Does the news focus on the negative in society? Why?

2. Is it good or bad to expose children to the news? Why or why not?

3. Why are some people "news junkies"?

4. Can watching the news make us numb to our surroundings? How?

5. Is there ever a time when governments should forbid or limit journalists from reporting "bad" news?

6. Do you believe the news is always true?

7. How does the media influence public opinion?

8. Which is the most influential – news from the newspaper, the radio, television, or the Internet?

9. How could reducing your attention to the news improve your health?

10. Does the news create feelings of despair and depression?

11. Should the news have more upbeat stories? Why?

12. What is the fastest way to spread the news?

QUESTIONS

B   The News

Tasks, page 119

13. Which is more important for you, local news or world news?	19. If someone leaks government secrets, should that be published as news?
14. How has the Internet changed people's exposure to news?	20. What kinds of activities that are newsworthy could you do at your school?
15. Can the news ever be unbiased?	21. Do you know any famous newscasters in the US? Why are they famous?
16. Should parents limit the amount of time a child spends watching the news?	22. If you could be on TV as a news personality, what part of the news would you want to report?
17. Would you like to be a reporter? Why or why not?	23. What kinds of topics do you feel are not newsworthy?
18. Why are a reporter's sources held confidential?	24. Is there any news that should not be reported to the public? What would that be?

A Obstacles/Disabilities

Tasks, page 120

QUESTIONS

QUESTIONS

1. Are there any obstacles in your life that have been difficult to overcome?

2. Do you ask for help when you face an obstacle in life? Who do you turn to?

3. Does your faith help you overcome problems in your life? How?

4. Have you or your child ever been bullied? What did you do?

5. Are little people discriminated against in this country?

6. Are you able to look beyond your immediate problems and still enjoy life?

7. If someone is depressed, is medication the answer?

8. Do you believe therapy can help a person overcome obstacles? How?

9. Can people with Down Syndrome lead a good life?

10. What are some obstacles you overcame to come to the US?

11. If you knew you were going to have a child with deformities or disabilities, would you consider aborting the fetus?

12. In your native country, are there any famous people who have overcome serious disabilities?

ProLinguaAssociates.com ◊ Photocopyable © 2020 Nancy Ellen Zelman

13. Do you or your family members have any disabilities?	19. Are there any physical disabilities you have overcome?
14. Which is more disabling, blindness or deafness?	20. Some disabled people consider themselves lucky. Why would they think so?
15. Do you know anyone with Asperger's or autism? How do they behave differently?	21. Have you ever witnessed someone making fun of someone with disabilities? Did you do anything?
16. What are some personality traits that can help a person overcome disabilities?	22. How did Helen Keller change the public's perception of disabilities?
17. Which would be more difficult to overcome, the inability to use your arms or your legs?	23. Why do some deaf people refuse to get hearing aids to help them hear better?
18. Is being a "special needs" child a disability?	24. Have you ever taken a sign language class? Why or why not?

QUESTIONS

Tasks, page 121

QUESTIONS

QUESTIONS

1. Do you ever lie?	7. What quality do you have that you are most proud of?
2. What have you lied about in your past?	8. Whom do you admire most in this country? In your native country?
3. Do you or your spouse forget important dates?	9. What do you worry about?
4. Have others ever teased you?	10. Do you generally like people? Do they usually like you?
5. Have you ever bullied others?	11. Do you prefer to know the truth even if it is bad, or to just not know?
6. What is the most important quality in a spouse?	12. Do you share your inner thoughts with anyone?

Tasks, page 121

13. Are you a pessimist or an optimist?	19. Are you a day or a night person?
14. Can you forgive and forget when someone does you wrong?	20. How do you get yourself motivated?
15. Are you persistent or do you give up easily?	21. When you are sad, do you stay with those feelings or do you try to be happy?
16. Are you a jack of all trades or do you have one thing you do well?	22. Is there anyone you look to for guidance?
17. Do you obsess about anything?	23. When was the last time you cried?
18. What frightens you?	24. Is there anyone or anything you would give your life for?

QUESTIONS

A Philanthropy

Tasks, page 122

1. What is the best charity to give to?	7. Do you give money to help animal welfare organizations? Why or why not?
2. Do you give more to others during the holidays?	8. Do you ever give money when people solicit on the phone?
3. Do you give to disaster relief funds?	9. Should religious organizations charge parishioners to belong?
4. How much money do you give to your religious institution?	10. Why do celebrities start their own foundations?
5. Why do so many people donate to charities anonymously?	11. Do you think celebrities should use their influence to support different causes?
6. What are some things we can do to "give back" to society?	12. Is volunteering in your community important to you?

B   Philanthropy

Tasks, page 122

QUESTIONS

13. If you had time to give, where would you volunteer?

14. Should schools require students to do community service in order to graduate?

15. What are the most popular charities in this country? In your native country?

16. Are there any charities you would not support?

17. Are there beggars in your native country?

18. What do you think of beggars who are begging with small children?

19. Have you ever picked up a worker who offered to work for food?

20. Do you stop to pick up hitchhikers? Why?

21. Would you hire someone from the street with a sign saying "Will work for food"?

22. If you died without any relatives, would you give your money to a charity? Which one?

23. Is there any hospital you would donate money to for research?

24. Would you ever partake in the "Ice Bucket Challenge" to raise money for ALS research?

QUESTIONS

Photocopyable © 2020 Nancy Ellen Zelman ◊ ProLinguaAssociates.com   **69**

Tasks, page 123

1. How do you like to party?	7. Do you prefer indoor or outdoor activities? Which ones?
2. Do you entertain people at your home?	8. Do you play card games?
3. Do you dance? What kind of dancing do you enjoy?	9. Do you prefer games on the computer or board games? Why?
4. Do you belong to a gym?	10. Have you ever gone camping? What do you like/ dislike about it?
5. Have you ever sung Kareoke?	11. How much money do you spend a year on hotels and motels?
6. Do you spend time at the library?	12. Do you prefer to watch movies at home or at the theater? Why?

QUESTIONS

QUESTIONS

13. What is a movie you will never forget? Why?	19. Do you ever bowl with your friends or family?
14. Who is an author you enjoy reading? Why?	20. How do you feel about the game of golf?
15. Do you ever cry at sad movies? Do you laugh out loud at funny movies?	21. Do you like the circus? Why?
16. Do you read any magazines or newspapers? Which do you enjoy?	22. Do you enjoy the rides at amusement parks? Which ones?
17. Do you make time to play with your loved ones? What do you play?	23. Have you been to any museums/art galleries in your community?
18. Do you read to anyone?	24. Do you go to concerts?

Q U E S T I O N S

A   Play 2

Q U E S T I O N S
Q U E S T I O N S

1. Have you ever been to a ballet?

2. When you are on vacation, do you take a lot of pictures?

3. Do you take more pictures of people or the sights?

4. What is your favorite thing to do on a vacation?

5. When you are on vacation, do you prefer to relax or sightsee?

6. What games did you play as a child that you don't play anymore?

7. Are there any games you played as a child that you taught your children?

8. Where do you like to hang out with friends?

9. Have you ever been to an opera?

10. What kinds of music do you enjoy?

11. Do you prefer live performances to those on TV or the Internet?

12. What kinds of rides do you like at amusement parks?

    ProLinguaAssociates.com   ◊   Photocopyable © 2020 Nancy Ellen Zelman

Tasks, page 123

13. Do you enjoy going to cafés or restaurants?	19. Would you ever parachute out of a plane for fun?
14. Have you ever been wine tasting?	20. Which of these sports would you like to learn: Surfing? Windsurfing? Skiing? Water skiing? Mountain climbing? Roller blading? Ice skating?
15. Would you prefer to play in the mountains or the ocean?	21. Do you ever go to comedy clubs?
16. Do you need a playmate to play or do you enjoy being alone?	22. Have you ever taken dancing lessons? If not, would you?
17. How many friends do you think is enough?	23. How much time each day should you set aside for fun?
18. Do you prefer to play with your friends or your family?	24. Do you have a hobby that you really enjoy?

QUESTIONS   QUESTIONS

Photocopyable © 2020 Nancy Ellen Zelman ◇ ProLinguaAssociates.com

A Race/Minorities

Tasks, page 124

1. Are there racial minorities in your native country?	7. Did you ever discriminate against a minority?
2. What are the racial problems you see in the US?	8. What causes racial prejudice?
3. Is it good to integrate schools by busing children? Why or why not?	9. Is there any way we can eliminate racial prejudice?
4. Where do many of the minorities in the US work? Where do they work in your country?	10. Is there a difference between someone who is an American black and someone who is an African black?
5. Does darker skin influence prejudice?	11. What is the politically correct way to refer to a person of color?
6. Do you prefer to socialize with people of your own color?	12. Is there a particular place where minorities live in this country? In your native country?

QUESTIONS

13. Why do so many people think racial minorities are dangerous?	**19.** Would you paint your face a different skin color?
14. Do any racial minorities hold elective office in your country?	**20.** Are some ethnicities better at basketball? Soccer? Track? Surfing? Why?
15. Has the election in the US of a black president changed people's racial prejudices?	**21.** Should the government give special treatment or money to certain minorities? Why?
16. Is it easier to be a white person or a black person in America? Why?	**22.** Why do minority groups tend to live together?
17. Are there any inborn differences between people of color and whites?	**23.** Are certain minorities discriminated against by the police in your country? In the US?
18. If you could have any color of skin, which would you choose? Why?	**24.** What are hate crimes? Should the crimes against minorities be more severely punished than other crimes? Why or why not?

A Sleep

QUESTIONS

1. How many hours do you sleep at night?	7. Do you prefer to sleep alone or with someone?
2. How many hours would you want to sleep each night?	8. What do you wear to sleep?
3. Have you ever slept through your alarm?	9. Can you sleep in any position?
4. What is your favorite sleeping position?	10. Do you ever wonder if you dreamed something or if it really happened?
5. Do you have a nightly ritual?	11. Have you ever had a recurring dream?
6. What do you do in order to help yourself fall asleep?	12. What kinds of pillows do you like? How many pillows do you sleep with?

QUESTIONS

B Sleep

13. In your native country, what do people prefer to sleep on?	19. What do you think of five-minute power naps? Would you be able to take a power nap at work?
14. Do you feel satisfied when you wake up or are you still tired?	20. Do you sleep through the night? What do you do if you can't fall asleep?
15. Have you ever had a nightmare you remembered for a long time?	21. Do you or your spouse snore?
16. Do you dream of falling or dying?	22. Does the room need to be dark for you to sleep?
17. Do you think dreams have meanings that we need to explore?	23. Do you like a soft or hard bed?
18. Do you take naps during the day?	24. Do you take any medication to help you sleep?

QUESTIONS

A Sports

Tasks, page 126

1. How important are sports in your life?	7. Do professional athletes get paid enough?
2. Would you want to be a professional athlete? Why or why not?	8. What are the pros and cons of professional sports?
3. Who is an athlete you admire greatly?	9. At what age should children be encouraged to join a sports team?
4. Why are sports important to children? To parents?	10. What is the role of a parent as a spectator of a child's sport?
5. What sports are too dangerous for children?	11. Is it more fun to watch a competition in person or on TV?
6. Does our society put famous athletes on a pedestal?	12. Why is there such an emphasis on winning a competition? Should we reward the winner and not the loser?

B   Sports

13. How can we teach children to be good losers?	**19.** Should girls and boys be on the same teams? Until what age?
14. Is it always possible to have good sportsmanship?	**20.** Is there enough supervision during sports events?
15. How can a parent support a child who aspires to be a famous athlete some day?	**21.** Are there any professional athletic teams you are a fan of?
16. What are extreme sports? Would you want to try any?	**22.** How many times a year do you go to professional sporting events?
17. What are the disadvantages of competitive sports?	**23.** Have you ever visited a sports museum?
18. How much practice or exercise is too much?	**24.** Do you have any memorabilia of a sports event?

QUESTIONS

A Taste

Tasks, page 127

QUESTIONS

1. Do you like spicy food? Salty food? Sweet food?

2. Which flavor of ice cream can you not get enough of?

3. Is there any ice cream flavor you would never eat?

4. Do you prefer sweet to salty?

5. What is the best dessert?

6. What is your favorite carbohydrate?

7. What condiments do you put on your food?

8. Do you drink a lot of soda? What kind?

9. Is there any fruit that is too sour to eat?

10. Do you eat raw cookie dough?

11. Do you watch cooking shows? Have you learned anything?

12. Do you chew gum? What flavor do you like best?

QUESTIONS

 ProLinguaAssociates.com ◊ Photocopyable © 2020 Nancy Ellen Zelman

QUESTIONS

13. Would you eat insects? What kind?	**19.** What drink do you usually order at a club or bar?
14. Is there any animal meat you would not eat?	**20.** Do you ever continue eating even when you are full?
15. If you wanted to lose weight, what would you cut out from your diet?	**21.** Is there any taste you cannot get enough of?
16. Could you be a vegetarian? A vegan?	**22.** Do you have a secret ingredient that you put into the foods you prepare?
17. Do you follow recipes when you cook, or do you make it up as you go along?	**23.** Are there any foods that are too spicy for you to eat?
18. Do you prefer to eat quality or quantity?	**24.** Are there any foods you wish you knew how to prepare?

QUESTIONS

A Technology 1

Tasks, page 128

1. Do you own your own computer?	7. Do you work in the Cloud and save data there? Why or why not?
2. Do you use a mouse on your computer?	8. Do you save photos on your computer? On your cell phone?
3. Does anyone other than you know your passwords?	9. Do you have any guards on your computer so that no one can hack your information?
4. How many different passwords do you have?	10. Do you allow your children use of your computer?
5. Do you play games on your computer? Which ones?	11. What applications could you not live without?
6. Do you prefer a Mac or a PC? Why?	12. Could you live for a week without your computer?

Tasks, page 128

QUESTIONS

13. Where do you go to get technical support?

14. What kind of cell phone do you have? Are you satisfied with it?

15. How many megabytes do you have on your cell phone?

16. At what age should a child be given a cell phone?

17. Have you ever broken your cell phone? How much would you spend to fix it?

18. Are there any advantages to having both a land line at home and a cell phone?

19. Are there advantages to having a pay-as-you-go cell phone?

20. Do you get cable TV or satellite?

21. Do you record any TV shows? Which ones?

22. What size TV do you have?

23. Do you prefer to watch movies in the theater, on TV, on your computer, or on your cellphone? Why?

24. Have you bought any apps for your phone? Which ones?

QUESTIONS

A Technology 2

Tasks, page 128

1. What search engine do you use?

2. What is the name of your email provider?

3. Do you mainly use your phone or a computer for the Internet?

4. Have you ever sold or bought anything from eBay?

5. Which shopping sites do you feel comfortable buying from?

6. Do you cruise the Internet and watch popular videos?

7. Do you buy music from iTunes?

8. Do you ever copy or download movies or songs illegally?

9. Do you use social networking to keep in touch with friends and family?

10. Do you prefer to talk to someone or text them?

11. Does it bother you when people text while they are having a conversation with you?

12. Have you ever texted in your car while driving?

13. Have you ever sent private information or photos to someone and later regretted it?	19. Have you ever waited in line to buy a technological device at a lowered price?
14. Have you ever posted anything on Youtube?	20. Is there any technology device that you are waiting to buy?
15. Do you ever take selfies and post them online?	21. Do you have a Twitter or Instagram account?
16. Do you skype anyone from your native country?	22. Do you follow any famous people on Twitter? Who and why?
17. Have you ever photo bombed a tourist taking a photo of a famous site?	23. Do you ever "like" or "not like" what someone posts? Explain.
18. How much money do you spend each month on your technological devices?	24. Have you ever blocked someone from texting you? Have you ever been blocked?

QUESTIONS

A Transportation

1. Have you ever been in a helicopter?

2. Do you like flying?

3. What kind of transportation do you think we will be using in the future?

4. How do you get to school/work?

5. Are the buses or metro in your city reliable?

6. What is the best part of riding a train?

7. Do you prefer to take a plane or a car if the distance to your destination is over 500 miles?

8. Is it less expensive to take a train or a bus?

9. Do you like to ride motorcycles?

10. When considering modes of transportation, which is more important to you, saving money or safety?

11. Which is more dangerous, a bicycle or a motorcycle?

12. Do you ride a bicycle? Do you use it for transportation or recreation?

 ProLinguaAssociates.com ◊ Photocopyable © 2020 Nancy Ellen Zelman

QUESTIONS

13. Do you ever take taxis? How much do you tip the driver?	**19. What do you do to equalize the air pressure in an airplane?**
14. Do you have a Metro in your country? Is it safe and convenient?	**20. Do you save frequent flyer miles?**
15. Would you be a passenger in a driverless vehicle?	**21. Have you ever used Uber? Is it economical and convenient?**
16. What do you do to pass time on an airplane?	**22. How does Uber affect the taxi industry?**
17. Are there enough air marshals on airplanes?	**23. Have you ever been in a limousine?**
18. Have you ever been on a boat? Do you get seasick?	**24. Do you feel safe taking public transportation?**

QUESTIONS

Photocopyable © 2020 Nancy Ellen Zelman ◇ ProLinguaAssociates.com

A Weather/Climate

Tasks, page 130

1. Do you prefer cold or hot weather?	7. Have you ever seen hail on a sunny day?
2. What is the weather like in your native country today?	8. Are you afraid of thunderstorms?
3. Do you depend on the weather forecast to dress for the day?	9. Which do you like more, thunder or lightning?
4. How do you deal with very hot weather?	10. What would the perfect weather for you be?
5. Do you dress in layers to prepare for the cold? What do you wear?	11. Do you like rain?
6. Does your hair respond to muggy weather? How?	12. Do you prefer to be in a downpour or a drizzle?

QUESTIONS

   ProLinguaAssociates.com ◊ Photocopyable © 2020 Nancy Ellen Zelman

B   Weather/Climate

Tasks, page 130

QUESTIONS

13. Is there snow in your native country? Where?

14. What do you like to do in the snow?

15. Do you prefer to be indoors or outdoors on a triple-digit day?

16. What do you think "June gloom" is? Do you have that in your native city?

17. Do you see various images in the clouds?

18. What is your favorite kind of cloud? Why?

19. Do you prefer mountain air or desert air?

20. If you could live in any climate in the world, where would you live?

21. How has climate change affected the world?

22. Do you think people can change the pace of global warming? How?

23. Are any animals or insects in danger of extinction because of global warming?

24. How does the weather affect your mood?

A Work

1. What is the best job to have?

2. Do you prepare for job interviews? How?

3. What is the best way to find a job?

4. What is the most profitable profession?

5. What do you wear for a job interview?

6. What do you like about your job?

7. Would you want your children to work at your job?

8. Would you work at your job for free to get experience?

9. Which is more important, on-the-job training or book knowledge?

10. Do you earn enough money for the work you do?

11. Do you prefer to work alone or with others?

12. What do you do when you disagree with your boss?

 ProLinguaAssociates.com ◊ Photocopyable © 2020 Nancy Ellen Zelman

B   Work

13. Do you speak English at your job? Why or why not?	**19. What classes do you wish you had taken to prepare yourself for the job market?**
14. Are there some jobs Americans will not do? Would you work at those jobs?	**20. What kinds of jobs will be obsolete in 5 years? 10 years? 50 years?**
15. Should we hire illegal aliens to do some jobs in this country? Why?	**21. What should the minimum wage be? Why?**
16. Should we punish employers who hire illegals? How?	**22. Does the US government give people enough money to survive when they are unemployed?**
17. At what age would you like to retire?	**23. What was the best job you ever had?**
18. Will you have enough money to retire?	**24. Do you feel fulfilled by your job? Why or why not?**

QUESTIONS

Advertising/Marketing

1. Design a label for a food product.

2. Design a full-page ad for a beverage.

3. Role-play a sales associate trying to sell a product to a customer who does not need the product.

4. Create a commercial for an automobile.

5. Present a reenactment of a bad commercial. Then enact how you would change it.

6. Make an advertisement for your school. Would it be a banner, a newspaper ad, an infomercial?

7. Design a web page for yourself advertising your attributes.

8. Make a label for yourself. What would your ingredients be?

ProLinguaAssociates.com ◊ Photocopyable © 2020 Nancy Ellen Zelman

Animals

<table>
<tr>
<td>

1. Research animal rescue groups in your area and share your information with the class.

</td>
<td>

5. Present a poster of your favorite pet.

</td>
</tr>
<tr>
<td>

2. Find out how to get a dog trained to assist the handicapped.

</td>
<td>

6. Look in magazines and prepare a collage of pictures of wild animals.

</td>
</tr>
<tr>
<td>

3. Find out which hospitals in your area bring in therapy animals.

</td>
<td>

7. Think of animals that interest you. Choose five that are similar in some way. Research them on line, and make a poster with pictures of them. See if the class can guess why you grouped them together.

</td>
</tr>
<tr>
<td>

4. Interview the owner of a therapy animal.

</td>
<td>

8. Volunteer at an animal rescue shelter. Take pictures and make a presentation to your class.

</td>
</tr>
</table>

TASKS

Appearance

T A S K S

1. Find pictures of the perfect face and present your findings to the class.

2. Find or create pictures of people wearing different clothing. Have the class guess the profession of these people based on their appearance.

3. Bring in clothing you have that you would wear for church, school, a job interview, or a party. Talk about them. How do they differ?

4. Research the salaries of successful models as compared with other professionals. Present your findings to the class and explain why the salaries are, or are not, justified.

5. Design your own anti-aging regime and present it to the class.

6. Interview five men and five women and ask them if they are happy or unhappy with their physical appearance. Find out what they like and dislike about how they look, and present your findings to the class.

7. Prepare your hair in a different style from the usual. Tell the class whether you feel any different.

8. Have each student draw a picture of either "what you looked like ten years ago" or "what you think you will look like ten years from now." Have the class match the pictures with the students.

T A S K S

Beliefs

T A S K S

1. Create a picture of what you think a space alien would look like.

2. Research psychic phenomena and present your findings to the class.

3. Bring in some typical good luck charms and explain them to the class.

4. Discuss a miracle you experienced.

5. Some people claim they live in haunted houses. Explain the reasons why these people believe their houses are haunted.

6. Research the marriage and divorce rates in the US and compare these with the rates in your native country.

7. Do a survey on whether people believe in love at first sight. Tell your class what you found out.

8. Compare five superstitions in your country to superstitions in the US.

T A S K S

Business

1. Write your resume.	5. Bring in a picture of a person you think would be hired for a professional job and explain why you think this based only on the person's appearance.
2. Prepare ten questions for a job interview. Ask another student the questions. Discuss whether you are satisfied with the answers.	6. Create a new company with a brand new product line.
3. Find a position advertised on Craigslist that you would be interested in applying for.	7. If you could hire anyone in the world to help you make a company successful, who would you hire? Bring in information about them, and explain why you would choose them.
4. As a boss, write down a list of ten things you are looking for in an applicant and explain to the class why these qualities are important.	8. Imagine you are firing several employees. Give them five reasons for your action.

 ProLinguaAssociates.com ◊ Photocopyable © 2020 Nancy Ellen Zelman

Cars and Drivers

Questions, page 12

1. Make a small model of your favorite car.	5. Find out which car is the most fuel economical. Compare it to the car which is the least economical and present to the class.
2. Make a poster of the history of automobiles.	6. Research classic cars or go to a car show. Tell the class about the most expensive car there and explain why its cost is so high.
3. Debate the pros and cons of traffic cameras.	7. Role-play a police officer and a driver who wants desperately to get out of paying a ticket.
4. Go to two new car dealerships. Take pictures of the cars you would never buy and explain to the class why they are undesirable.	8. Design the car of the future. Make a diorama and present to the class.

TASKS

Chores

1. Choose one household chore and explain the procedure for doing it well.	5. Compare household chores in your native country and the US. Are they the same? Draw a picture illustrating a difference, and explain it to the class.
2. Bring in some common household products and sell the products in front of the class.	6. Make a poster or diorama of your home and the tools and appliances that make doing chores easier.
3. Compare an environmentally friendly household product to a non-friendly product.	7. Research a valuable household appliance. Discuss its history and what other appliances or tools it replaced.
4. Design a household appliance that would improve your life.	8. Take a survey in your class. Find out which chores are the most liked and the most hated.

 ProLinguaAssociates.com ◊ Photocopyable © 2020 Nancy Ellen Zelman

Communication

1. Research the design of the phone from the past to the present. Draw pictures to show the progression.	5. Write a letter to your best friend or family member in your native country. Mail it.
2. Call three people from your class and have a conversation in English for three minutes with each of them. Tell the class about your conversations.	6. Whisper an English sentence to a classmate. Then have your partner whisper the secret to another classmate until all classmates have heard the sentence. The last student writes the sentence on the board.
3. Learn the alphabet in sign language and then teach the alphabet to the class.	7. Make a crossword puzzle using vocabulary in the "Question" part of this unit.
4. Role-play a telephone conversation complaining about a product you bought.	8. Count the minutes you are on the phone or texting each day. After one week, bring in your record and compare it to other classmates.

T A S K S

Crime/Punishment

1. Imagine you are a police officer. Explain to the class why it is a good job.

2. Prepare a debate to argue the pros and cons of legalizing marijuana.

3. Role-play a traffic stop. Explain to the officer why you do not deserve a ticket.

4. Research which states in the US have capital punishment.

5. Read the police log in your local newspaper. Summarize it for your class.

6. Visit a government office and tell your class about it.

7. Explain five reasons why you would not want to be a lawyer, and five reasons why you would like to.

8. Do some research on the jail and juvenile hall in your community. Explain your findings to the class.

Current Events / Politics

Questions, page 20

1. In a newspaper, magazine, or on the internet, read a current events article and summarize it. Explain why you think your source was or was not telling the truth.

2. Do a collage of the week's current events.

3. Find out how we can predict natural disasters.

4. Explain to the class how to protect themselves from the next natural disaster.

5. Research loss of life from an ongoing conflict abroad.

6. Prepare a roundtable UN discussion on how to solve the world's economic problems.

7. Have a presidential debate. What would you base your platform on? Is it important to be polite/civil?

8. Create a list of how the US could improve immigration laws.

Customs/Holidays

Questions, page 22

1. Bring in a costume that is traditional in your country and explain it to the class.

2. Demonstrate a traditional dance from your country.

3. Translate the words of your national anthem and explain to the class the significance of the anthem.

4. Bring in several items that you brought to the US from your country. Explain their value to you to your class.

5. Create a poster showing the differences between a holiday in your native country and a holiday in the US.

6. Bring in a typical dish from your country and share it with the class.

7. Bring in some artifact from your native country. See if the class can guess what it is or the purpose it serves.

8. Bring in a recipe and the ingredients for a typical meal in your country. Explain to the class how to make the dish.

 ProLinguaAssociates.com ◊ Photocopyable © 2020 Nancy Ellen Zelman

Daily Rituals

Questions, page 24

T A S K S

1. Act out a day in your life as your classmates describe what you're doing.

2. Take pictures of a day in your life. Explain the pictures to your class.

3. Ask your partner questions and then draw a series of pictures depicting your partner's daily rituals.

4. Make a poster of a typical day in your life.

5. Write down your most unusual daily ritual. Put it in a "pot" with others, and then guess who wrote which ritual.

6. In a group, make up 20 yes/no questions that you could ask to find out about a person's daily routine. Compare your group's questions to the questions of another group. As a class, choose the 20 best overall questions.

7. Interview someone not in your family. Ask them how they spend a typical day. Compare their day to yours.

8. Find out about gym memberships in your neighborhood. Explain why it is better either to join a gym for exercise or to work out at home.

T A S K S

Photocopyable © 2020 Nancy Ellen Zelman ◊ ProLinguaAssociates.com

Dating/Marriage

T A S K S

1. Write a profile you could use on a dating site.

5. Make a presentation about marriage customs and rituals in your country and compare them to those of the US.

2. Role-play a blind date.

6. Describe a perfect date.

3. Research polygamy in the US. Do any states tolerate this? Why?

7. Are humans naturally monogamous? Research and discuss.

4. Make a list of dating shows on television. Which shows are more realistic?

8. Ask your classmates: Is it easier to be a woman or a man on a date? Discuss or debate.

T A S K S

Death

1. Read a few obituaties and tell the class how to write one. Write your own obituary.	5. Do a poster reflecting the process of life from birth to death.
2. Find out from your class-mates if they have made arrangements for their final resting place.	6. Find out about life insur-ance and compare the costs and benefits.
3. Research five countries and find out about their burial ceremonies.	7. Visit an old cemetery in your community. Take photos of some of the interesting gravestones and share the pictures with your class.
4. Talk for five minutes about someone you knew who has died.	8. Talk about a near-death experience and share it with a partner.

Education

T A S K S

1. Design a curriculum for this class.

2. Create a pay scale for teachers at your school.

3. Make a diorama of the perfect classroom.

4. Write and present your reasons for or against arming teachers at your school.

5. Make signs against bullying that you can post around a school.

6. Make a list of things your school needs or could benefit from having. Compare your list to that of your classmates.

7. Make a list of the best qualities in a teacher.

8. Interview two people, asking them who their favorite teacher was and why.

T A S K S

Environment/Ecology

Questions, page 32

1. Make a poster depicting the change in a region's climate over the decades.

2. Research animals that are now extinct, and prepare a report on the reasons for this.

3. Seek out the closest animal sanctuary; find out what animals it protects and why.

4. Research fuel-efficient cars. Which would save the most money for a consumer over the course of five years?

5. Take a poll and find out if people would pay more money to buy products that do not hurt the environment. How much more money would they pay?

6. Start a recycling program in your school.

7. Create posters encouraging people to recycle.

8. Make sure your classroom and home have emergency plans in case of disasters. Review them and explain them to your class.

Family

1. Bring in pictures of your family. Mix them up in a pile with pictures from other students' families and try to guess which pictures go with which student.

2. Make a family tree of your ancestry.

3. Watch some TV shows depicting families. Explain to the class which show most closely exemplifies your family and why.

4. Have a party and invite the families of your classmates.

5. Bring in items given to you by family members; explain why these items are important to you.

6. Write a paragraph about your family telling how much you love them.

7. Interview some of your relatives. Find out what for them is the most important thing about family.

8. If you could have anyone join your family, who would you invite? Explain your choice to your class.

ProLinguaAssociates.com ◊ Photocopyable © 2020 Nancy Ellen Zelman

Fashion

1. Create a fashion show for your class using your classmates as models. Explain their outfits.

2. Go to the thrift shops in your neighborhood. Create a fashionable outfit spending only five dollars. Model it for your class.

3. Create a poster showing the different fads that are in fashion and out of fashion.

4. Cut out pictures of celebrities wearing outfits that you like and don't like. Share them with the class.

5. Find pictures of clothing you would buy if you had unlimited funds. Research and see if you can find similar fashions at affordable prices.

6. Find pictures of traditional clothing in your country. Have a Show and Tell with your class.

7. What is your favorite piece of clothing? Bring it in and tell the class why you like it.

8. Take pictures of different kinds of footwear. Make a poster, bring it in, and ask your classmates to explain which they like the best and why.

TASKS

Favorites/Least Favorites

Questions, page 38

1. Bring in several of your favorite things and share with your class.

2. Bring in several of your least or most favorite childhood toys and mix them in the middle of the room with other students' least (most) favorites. Try to match the students and their toys.

3. Find the music and words to the song "My Favorite Things." Distribute the words to the class. Call on your classmates to explain any vocabulary. Then sing along with a recording.

4. Interview five men and five women outside your class. Ask them all the same question and find out if there are any similar answers. Report your findings to the class.

5. Find five songs on the Internet that have the words "favorite" or "least favorite." Present the lyrics to the class.

6. Make a list of colors. Rank them from your favorite to your least favorite. Compare your list to other lists in the class.

7. Make a poster showing your least favorite (or favorite) things.

8. Make five questions about favorite and least favorite things. Poll the students in the class. Find out which students share some favorites and least favorites.

Food

1. Have a party and prepare a food from your country to present to your friends.

2. Blindfold a student and see if they can guess the vegetable or fruit they are tasting.

3. Play Liars Club: Bring in an unusual food or spice. Give three possible names for it and have students guess which is correct.

4. Find out how many calories are in a serving of several popular fast food items. Explain to the class what you learned and how you learned it.

5. Do a taste test comparing some organic and non-organic food and see if there is a taste difference.

6. Find pictures of different foods and recipes. Have students match the pictures of each food with the correct recipe.

7. Create a menu for a party at your home.

8. Bring in a menu from a restaurant in your neighborhood. Exchange menus with other students and compare them.

Photocopyable © 2020 Nancy Ellen Zelman ◊ ProLinguaAssociates.com

Gender / Sex

Questions, page 42

T A S K S

1. Choose a famous man if you are a woman, or woman if you are a man. Do a report on how this person became famous and present your report to the class.

2. Create 20 questions for a survey about gender. Distribute the survey to both women and men and tally the differences in their answers based on gender.

3. Research the leaders of your native country in the last 50 years. Explain to the class why one gender is more prevalent.

4. Make a list of six professions in the US. Use the Internet to research the percentages of men and women in these professions.

5. Choose a country you know very little about. Research to find out if this country has different laws for men and women.

6. Create a collage that typifies stereotypes of men and women.

7. In small groups, discuss the important attributes of men and women. Make a list of these attributes. Compare what you have with another group.

8. Role-play a situation in which a girl is bullied at school by boys. Then role-play a boy being bullied by boys. Discuss with the class how the responses from a girl and boy differ.

T A S K S

Health

TASKS

1. Research the cost of a checkup at three different medical practices and report to the class what you found.	5. Role-play a doctor and patient. The doctor can only spend a limited time with the patient, but unfortunately the patient has a lot of maladies.
2. Create a list of the vitamins and food supplements you take daily. Exchange the list with a classmate and explain why you take them.	6. Bring in and discuss some homeopathic cures.
3. Research the differences in the cost of a specific drug at five different pharmacies.	7. Find out from your relatives what home remedies they have. Explain them to your class.
4. Find out how many years of schooling and experience your doctor/dentist has.	8. Research home remedies for common maladies on the Internet and present your findings to the class.

TASKS

Home

T A S K S

1. Take several pictures of the inside and outside of your house and share them with your classmates.

2. Be an architect. Design the ideal home for you and your family.

3. Bring in pictures from magazines showing how you would change your house if money was not an issue.

4. Explain to the class how your home in your native country differed from the home you have now.

5. Create a diorama of the favorite room in your house.

6. Find out from members of your family which room in the house they would like to change. Work together to improve it.

7. Make a collage of beautiful houses you would love to own.

8. Research the home of a famous person. Explain to the class why you would or wouldn't want to live in that house.

T A S K S

Issues

T A S K S

1. In small groups, make a list of ten issues. Individually express your opinions about each one.

2. In pairs, one student takes the pro side of an issue while the other takes the con. Present the two sides to the class.

3. Hold a formal debate on one of the issues.

4. Stage a talk show with panelists giving different opinions on an issue.

5. Make a collage supporting one of your opinions.

6. Take turns giving a three-minute ad lib opinion about an issue.

7. Write a skit showing how a hero could save the country from a terrorist.

8. Take a poll of your classmates as to whether they feel safe or in danger around police officers. Tell the class your results and explain why you think you got those results.

Love

T A S K S

1. In groups, prepare a wedding ceremony from one of your native countries and present it to the class.

2. Bring in photos of your wedding and share them.

3. Discuss the meaning of platonic love.

4. Discuss how animals show love to other animals and to people.

5. Role-play a situation where you are the parent and you meet one of your daughter's dates. Ask him questions.

6. Write wedding vows.

7. In a small group, brainstorm the many kinds of love.

8. Find five songs with the word "Love" in the title. Copy the lyrics and distribute them to the class. Have the class decide which song best exemplifies the idea of love.

T A S K S

Money / Finance

T A S K S

1. Show the rest of your class how much money you brought to school for lunch or dinner, and explain what you plan to eat.

2. Bring in bills for utilities and compare them with other students' bills.

3. Role-play how you would persuade a family member to lend you money.

4. Make a list of the benefits of using cash, credit, or checks. Explain to the class why you use what you do.

5. With a classmate or classmates compare credit cards. Which do you think are best and why?

6. Research the rewards programs of different credit cards and present your findings.

7. Research who the wealthiest person in the world is and how he got his money.

8. Research the minimum wage in three countries. Explain to the class why you think each wage is sufficient or insufficient.

T A S K S

Native Country

T A S K S

1. **Bring in pictures of famous sites in your native city.**

2. **Research someone who is famous in your country and share your findings with the class.**

3. **Make a list of five things you would want to change in your country.**

4. **Write a new law you would like to see enacted in your native country.**

5. **Make a poster with pictures of your native country.**

6. **Create a travel brochure for tourists to your country.**

7. **Make a list of warnings for travelers to your country.**

8. **Have an international day. Set up a booth from your country for others to visit.**

T A S K S

 ProLinguaAssociates.com ◊ Photocopyable © 2020 Nancy Ellen Zelman

The News

Questions, page 62

1. Create a newspaper for your school.

2. Work with other students and create a five-minute TV news commentary.

3. Research pop news in the US and present your findings to the class.

4. Bring in a newspaper article and present it to the class.

5. Summarize a current news item each day for two weeks. Exchange with another student in the class.

6. Bring in items that could be used for a time capsule exemplifying the times. Share them with your class.

7. Create a poster of this week's news.

8. Research a famous news reporter. Present your person to the class.

Obstacles/Disabilities

Questions, page 64

1. Do a report on a famous American who overcame a physical disability.

2. Write twenty questions you would like to ask a teacher of children with "special" needs. Interview a teacher and report to the class.

3. Find out what jobs are available for people with special needs in your community.

4. Write a report on myths associated with people with disabilities.

5. Find out if there are any television shows representing people with special needs and share what you find out with the class.

6. Research "autism" on the Internet. Explain the spectrum.

7. Give a speech explaining whether it is more debilitating to have a mental disability or a physical one.

8. Find out about savants and report your findings to the class.

 ProLinguaAssociates.com ◊ Photocopyable © 2020 Nancy Ellen Zelman

Personal

T A S K S

1. Research character traits. Make a list of twenty words about character that you do not know. Find them in a dictionary and present the new vocabulary to your class.	5. Choose a famous person and read about them. Make a list of that person's opinions. Have a partner then read your list and create a true/false quiz. Give the quiz to the class; then show them your list and discuss the correct answers.
2. Choose one important character trait that you admire in others. Make a poster with pictures and words depicting this trait.	6. All students write twenty sentences about themselves, but do not put their names on their lists. They put all their papers in a "pot," and then try to guess which student in the class wrote which list.
3. Make signs showing how people should or should not behave toward one another. Share your signs with those of your classmates, and choose ten signs to put up around your school.	7. In a small group, each person names someone famous. Then they tell each other how they feel about the famous people chosen.
4. Imagine you are writing an autobiography. Write down several titles for your book.	8. Imagine you and your group are giving out the Nobel Peace Prize. Decide together who would receive the award and who would get second and third place honors.

Philanthropy

Questions, page 68

1. Look through your clothes and call local thrift stores to schedule a donation.	5. Make a list of the organizations in your community that need volunteers. Prioritize the list starting with those most in need, and post the list at your school.
2. Research the best organizations to give money to. Present your findings to the class.	6. Interview local volunteers. Find out why they do what they do without pay. Report to the class on their work, using photos if possible.
3. Find out about your local food bank and what food is needed. Collect these items from your school for donation.	7. Talk to someone working in a volunteer organization. Invite them to come to your class and explain their work. Does the organization need more volunteers?
4. Volunteer to spend time helping the needy in your neighborhood.	8. Organize people in your community to volunteer to clean up your school or your neighborhood.

Play

1. Invite a classmate to join you after class for some fun.	5. Explain to a classmate how to do something you do well that your classmate has never done.
2. Try something that you have never done before for recreation, and then present your experience to the class.	6. Talking for three minutes, try to convince a classmate to try something they have never done before.
3. Make a poster on your favorite fun activity.	7. Get a brochure on camps in your community.
4. Get a group of your classmates who have never done an activity to go and do the activity together.	8. Find out the times and prices for various movies in your neighborhood.

Race/Minorities

1. Research and report on minorities in the US.	5. Give a presentation to the class about when you or your family member experienced discrimination.
2. Make a poster on the "melting pot" aspect of the US.	6. Find out where ethnic minorities live in your city. Bring a map showing the neighborhoods where they live.
3. Find pictures of the different shades of skin and create a poster showing the spectrum.	7. Make up five questions to ask people about their prejudices and views on prejudice. Take a poll and ask these questions to ten men and ten women. Tell the class about your findings.
4. Do a report on someone like Nelson Mandela who overcame racial prejudice and how that person overcame it.	8. Interview a person who is gay, lesbian, or transgender. Take notes on what their experience has been and explain it to the class.

TASKS

 ◇ Photocopyable © 2020 Nancy Ellen Zelman

Sleep

1. Keep a journal of your dreams for one week.	5. Research the biological need for sleep and present your findings to the class.
2. Keep a record for two weeks of the time you go to sleep and what you think about before you fall asleep.	6. Look on the Internet and find out creative ways to fall asleep.
3. Role-play someone who is woken up by noisy neighbors.	7. Make a list of ways to help someone when they wake up in the middle of the night and can't fall back asleep.
4. Take a poll of your classmates asking how many hours a night they sleep.	8. Prepare a speech on a dream you have had more than once. Give you speech to the class.

TASKS

Sports

Questions, page 70

1. Attend a professional sports event that you have never been to before.	5. Bring in some sports equipment. Blindfold a classmate and have them guess what item you brought and the sport it is used in.
2. Find out from your classmates who has children engaged in a sport. Go to their sporting event.	6. Without speaking, act out a sport and have your classmates guess which sport it is.
3. Try a sport that you have never tried before.	7. Choose a sport. In one minute, draw pictures on the board representing the sport and have your classmates guess the sport.
4. Teach your classmates how to play a sport they have never tried.	8. Do a report on a famous athlete.

TASKS

TASKS

Taste

T A S K S

1. Bring in examples of salty, bitter, sour, and sweet foods. Have your classmates close their eyes and only by smelling, guess which is which.

2. Bring in a sample of a favorite food. Blindfold your partner and have them guess what food it is.

3. Make a poster of the many different spices and foods in your native country.

4. Bring in samples of popular spices in your native country and share them with the class.

5. Have a potluck party and taste a little of everything your friends prepare.

6. Research the different kinds of hot peppers. Bring examples to your class and see which student can eat the hottest pepper without water.

7. Explain to the class why you are or are not a foodie.

8. Watch two different cooking shows. Make a list of how the shows are similar and different.

T A S K S

Photocopyable © 2020 Nancy Ellen Zelman ◊ ProLinguaAssociates.com

Technology

Questions, pages 82-85

T A S K S

1. **Find out how to rent a textbook online.**	5. **Design a computer of the future.**
2. **Find a funny video online and share it with your class.**	6. **Do not use cell phones or computers for one week. Write a report on how this changed your daily life.**
3. **Explain to a classmate the features of your cell phone.**	7. **Research online the history of the computer. Make a poster showing how the computer has evolved.**
4. **Research the kinds of computers that were popular twenty years ago and compare them to our modern computers.**	8. **Write a step-by-step process in which you can explain to someone how to find something using a search engine.**

T A S K S

 ProLinguaAssociates.com ◊ Photocopyable © 2020 Nancy Ellen Zelman

Transportation

1. In groups, discuss ways to reduce traffic congestion and pollution.	5. Describe where you would go on a hot air balloon ride. Bring pictures and share with the class.
2. Do a collage on modern transportation.	6. Design a trip across the US. Show your route and explain your modes of transportation.
3. Compare several airlines and their frequent flier mileage for a round trip ticket to your native country and back.	7. Research how the train has changed in the last fifty years and present your findings to the class.
4. Take a loop ride on the bus. Bring in a map and describe the route.	8. Tell the class about a boat ride you have taken.

T A S K S

T A S K S

Photocopyable © 2020 Nancy Ellen Zelman ◇ ProLinguaAssociates.com

Weather/Climate

Questions, page 88

1. Make believe you are a weatherperson on television and give a one-minute report on your prediction for tomorrow's weather.

2. Research how weather in your community has changed over the past ten years.

3. Interview five people in your community and find out if they think there has been climate change there.

4. Do a collage on the weather in each season.

5. Find out what to do in different weather emergencies. Present your findings to the class.

6. On the Internet, find twenty words relating to weather that you do not know. Present these words to the class, making sample sentences using them.

7. Teach the class how to convert Celsius to Fahrenheit and vice versa.

8. Do research on how global warming has influenced the weather in your area. Present your findings to the class.

Work

1. Find an after-school job that you could apply for.	5. In the newspaper, find 5 jobs you would like to have. Explain why these jobs would suit you.
2. Research what companies in your neighborhood have job openings, and present your findings to the class.	6. Go to five restaurants or stores in your neighborhood and ask each for a job application.
3. Make up 20 job interview questions you would ask a potential employee. With a classmate, practice asking and answering your questions.	7. Explain to the class how much money you would need per hour to survive comfortably.
4. Explain to the class your ideal job.	8. Write a speech on the best and the worst job you have had. Present it to the class.

TASKS

Other Pro Lingua Books
for Practicing

Conversation and Discussion Skills

Conversation Inspirations by Nancy Ellen Zelman

In My Opinion by Phil Keegan

Faces by Patrick R. Moran

Thinking Deeper by John Spiri

Conversation Strategies
Discussion Strategies
Basic Conversation Strategies
by David Kehe and Peggy Dustin Kehe

Business Communication Strategies
by Scott Smith

Dictations for Discussion
Interactive Dictations
Great Dictations
Basic Dictations
by Catherine Sadow and Judy DeFilippo

Dictation Riddles by Jane Gragg Lewis

Bumper Sticker by Arthur A. Burrows

Lessons on Life, Learning, and Leadership
for Reading, Thinking, and Discussing by Brian Reamer

These and other books that build conversation skills
are available at ProLinguaAssociates.com